LYFE N MY STILETTO

I0115974

LYFE N MY STILETTOS

Laqulia Shinn

LYFE N MY STILETTOS

ISBN:0615763162
ISBN:9780615763163

LYFE N MY STILETTOS

DEDICATION

To the Shinn Family, Sims Family, Stroud Family, Lewis Family, Sulphur Springs Missionary Baptist Church, My one and only best friend Dianna Jefferson, and Especially my children: Saddiyia, Derek Jr., Keasia.

CONTENTS

LYFE N MY STILETTOS

ACKNOWLEDGMENTS

I would like to thank God first and foremost for his grace and mercy bestowed upon me not only on this long journey to me finding my inner faith, but for keeping me all the years I was lost and drowning in sin. To God, all my praise and glory is due.

I definitely wouldn't be here or be the woman I am today without my momma and this long road we have been riding on for 27 years, which has brought joy, pain, tears, smiles, growth, and knowledge. "I love you momma"

To all my family members, I recognize the love. Thanks for putting up with me for 27 long years. I love each of you the same. Despite past stumbling block, we will continue to rise as long as God is 1st.

(SSSL)

To my best friend, "My Ride or Die" Dianna Jefferson, words can't explain our friendship or the love I have for you. "I love you sis. This is only the beginning"

Also, to my church family at Sulphur Springs Missionary Baptist Church in Hamilton, MS, under the leadership and love of Reverend Henry Mosley; I love my pastor, because he is a true man of God and he has always encouraged me to keep on keeping on.

To everyone that supported me and encouraged me not to throw in the towel; in my heart there will always be a great deal of respect and love for y'all.

Last, but definitely not least, my lifelines: Saddiyia, Derek Jr., and Keasia. Y'all are the reason mommy never gave up on her dreams. I don't ever want y'all to ever think of giving up on anything. The three of you can do anything you put your minds to! As long as I got air in my body, momma will make sure y'all never have to want for anything y'all need and most of things y'all want. "L.S.D.K.4"

1 INTRODUCTION

Growing up in Mississippi as a black child in a low poverty level family, I saw things that removed the illusions of life. Watching my grandmother, mother, aunts, and cousins settle for less in every aspect of life: men, jobs, education, and abuse beyond measure turned-on a light in my nine year old head. I watched my mother experience different relationships and become physically abused by the one man I ever knew to love her. The abusive atmosphere place in me an unbearable fear of relationships and instilled a distrust of men.

I remember it like it happened yesterday; "I will never let a man put his hands on me or I'm gone kill his ass." I thought. As a child I thought I could predict the future of my dreams and lifestyle, but I soon learned what God really had in store for the little nine year old.

2 BEGINNINGS

It's kind of funny how Dee and I came to be friends. Dee and her family moved to Caledonia in 1998 if I remember correctly. The first time I saw her I said to myself, "She think she's all that." I automatically didn't like her of course, because she was the new girl on the block or should I say "school." Dee came off as a quiet, self-centered person... We had gym class together and on our first day in gym class together, I had already established that I didn't like her and I wanted to fight her. I was just an evil bully. As tiny as I was, who would think I could intimidate and control so many people. I inherited popularity due to the largeness and background of my family. I approached Dee about 30 minutes into class and said to her "I heard you didn't like me and you wanted to fight me?" Dee was looking clueless to the fact and knew right off I was lying and that I was just trying to start a fight with her. She said "Who said I didn't like you? And why would I want to fight you? I don't even know you." I said some other smart remarks and I walked away. After a few weeks in gym class together and really observing her, I started to feel bad about trying to pick a fight with her. I'm not sure exactly how we began talking to each other after the altercation we had. It probably was me, because that heifer is more stubborn than me! All I know, After all the beef between us passed, we became inseparable! Dee and I dated two guys who were best friends just like we were. We would sneak off during the weekends and during school to meet with them. Our relationships with them brought us a lot of joy and pain, but until this day, Dee and I have their hearts in our pockets and they'll tell you that...

All though I had a challenging, painful, unforgettable past, I can honestly say I never stop fighting for a better tomorrow. I never gave up hope on a brighter future. I knew that it was possible for me to have the life I saw for myself as a child, and the only way to obtain it was to put my trust in God. I must give credit to my grandma "Madea" for making us go to church even if we didn't want to go to church. The bible says, "Train up a child in the way they should go, and they won't depart from it." I don't know about anybody else, but as for me that's a true Statement. Because it didn't matter how far I strayed away from church when I got older; I always found my way back to the church, even if it wasn't my hometown church. It's something about hearing the word of God that kept me, uplifted me, and saved me. After straying away from God's word for over a decade, in August 2012 I found myself in my hometown church "Sulphur Springs Missionary Baptist Church." Revival week, front and center at the altar, crying out and calling out for God to forgive me for my sins and wipe my slate clean, I remember the tears over lapping on my face. I was so weak... all I could do was say, "Lord, I'm sorry. I'm nothing but a filthy rag, but if you clean me up, I will serve you the rest of my days." That was five months ago and by the grace of God, I am still holding on and I am still standing on his word. This year by itself has challenged me to take back control over my life, and ever since I turned my life back over to the Lord things have not been the same. Everything I touch prospers. Everything I speak comes to past. I know that I'm walking in the favor of God, and let me tell you something. "When you're walking in God's favor, there ain't anything anyone can do to stop you from prospering." All I want to do is the will of God and keep his ten commandments. Who would have known that I would become the Founder of an "All-Girl Youth Ministry?" God's plans for me are unfolding in front of my very eyes, and I am beyond grateful! The "Rising Star's All-Girl Youth Ministry is going to take my community, city, and state by surprise.

In March 2012, I moved to Pensacola to reunite with my best friend Dee Jefferson. Dee decided that she wanted to live in Orlando, Florida, so we both applied for jobs in Pensacola and Orlando. I was kind of reluctant at first; but after analyzing everything that was going on in my life, I figured, what the heck could it hurt by going to Orlando. We planned to go to Orlando for a week and return to Pensacola. After being in Orlando the first three days, we knew we needed to extend our deadline.

We lived in a hotel until our money started running low. Dee's car was our next Orlando home, which we called "Betty-Ann." Then and now, people ask us "Why in the world would y'all stay in Orlando and live in a car, when y'all could have easily went back to Dee apartment in the Pensacola?" I always tell them, "We were tired of running back and given up on things. We stuck together and we encouraged each other to stay strong and hold on, because God didn't guide us there to leave us." Within a week we had several job offers; some good jobs and some bad jobs. We each accepted the good jobs.

Moving to Orlando and living in Orlando was a big part of a new direction in my life. Dee and I often talked about how our lives changed drastically after high school. I graduated from Douglassville High School in Atlanta and Dee graduated from a high school in Indiana. She moved to Pensacola; I stayed in Atlanta, leaving our friendship to survive on its own. During our separation of almost 10 years we hardly ever communicated or visited each other due to the traveling distance.

The day I decided to write "Lyfe in my Stilettos," Dee and I were sitting at the library in Orlando, Florida. Why did I decide to write this book? I decided to write "Lyfe in My Stilettos" in order to help young men and women change their thought process and make the life changes necessary for success.

3 DECISIONS

Deciding not to attend college right after high school was one of my biggest mistakes. My mom decided to move back to Mississippi, where I was born and raised, but I did not want to move. I was in a relationship with my high school sweetheart Tavarus Waller; we were madly in love! Moving in with Tavarus and his mom solved my immediate problem.

In the beginning, Tavarus had the best attitude and personality of any guy I'd ever met. He opened doors for me and gave me his coat if we were out and it started raining. He was the perfect guy. I thought we would be together forever.

Tavarus is tall with a light skin complexion. He had very long black curly hair which was always braided back. He had the prettiest big smile, beautiful brown eyes, and a long pointed nose like my Uncle Walter.

When I first met Tavarus, I was strongly attracted to him. He loved to play basketball with his homeboys and the other guys in the apartment community. He was so sweet back then. Most important, we were friends before we became lovers. I guess we should have remained friends, because we no longer communicate without arguing and bringing up past issues. Our relationship is so unhealthy. All I can do is pray that we one day regain our friendship or at least a good communication relationship for the kids' sake.

Just thinking back on all that I went through with Tavarus still brings tears to my eyes. I remember after having our first child and only a few days after getting out the hospital, we had an argument about something and he completely lost it. He dragged me down the stairs, while I was only wearing a bra and panties. I was screaming and crying at the top of my lungs for him to stop! Not only did he refuse to stop, when we reached the bottom of the stairs, he threw me out the front door. He then hit me a couple of times, and locked me out of the house. With my eyes full of tears, completely embarrassed and heartbroken, I had no choice but to walk to my neighbor's house to use the phone. My neighbors were completely upset and ashamed for me. He wouldn't let me get my baby or anything, and he told me he'd kill me if I ever tried to take her away from him. How could a man be so cruel to the mother of his children?

Out of all the abuse I endured while I was with Tavarus, that day sticks out in my brain like a sore thumb. He broke my heart so bad. I was terrified of him and felt like everything that happened to me was my fault. For years I allowed him to demolish my character, self-esteem, and mind. I thought I would never get the strength to leave him, but I did. It was only by the grace and mercy of my God!

4 BORN INTO IT

I was born October 5, 1985 in Columbus, Mississippi to Mary Ann Shinn and Mike Lee Stephen. At the time, my Momma thought that my daddy was someone else. Well, I don't want say "thought." I'll just say she wished that I was the daughter of the love of her life, James Porter, but she knew the truth. The timing of my birth didn't add up, and she hated it.

I spent most of my childhood living in Caledonia and Columbus. Columbus is considered the city and Caledonia of course is the country, with the majority of its residents being white people. As a child, I can remember being so spoiled and loved. I always got my way because I was very sensitive, meaning I cried about any and everything. If someone even hollered at me, I cried. My feelings were very easy to hurt. I was born into a very large family. My grandma, Madea is the mother of sixteen children, ten daughters and six sons. My grandpa (Pa Pa) had three sons born to my grandmother. My great grandma, my grandma's mother, had seventeen children, fourteen sons and three daughters.

My mom is the mother of seven children, four daughters and three sons. I am the eldest daughter. My brother Rico is the second child. He is now twenty-five years old, and has a five year old daughter Jayla (La-La). She is truly his twin. My niece La-La, whom I love so much, is super smart and adorable. My brother was known to be very hyperactive. He aggravated everybody all the time. It seemed to me that he was just seeking attention and behaved badly to get the attention. Rico, like many other black males I know, fell victim to the streets of Mississippi and is currently serving time in Wilkerson County Prison here in the state.

Tonio who is my mom's third born child is the only one out of my mama's sons who is out in the "free world." As a child, he never really talked to anyone and didn't care too much for socializing. He is the quiet one out of all my siblings; he keeps to himself, but at times he can definitely get under my skin. Although all of my brothers are "Mama Boys," Tonio loved playing football and watching wrestling. He is also the only one of my siblings who doesn't have any kids, but he always says he wants 13 boys. I think that's just crazy.

My sister Chyna is the second born daughter of my mother. Chyna is completely different from the rest of us. She is very self-enclosed. As a child, she often kept to herself. She also fought all of the time and had low self-esteem, which resulted in a very bad temper. She was and still is the "evil child;" meaning she never says anything if you mess with her, but we always say, "You better not go to sleep."

Like Dee and I, Chyna completely changed and turned her life around. She went from being this low self-esteem, angry child and teenager to a wonderful, determined, self-motivated, woman. She is a Certified Nursing Assistant who works at a nursing home in Amory, Mississippi. She doesn't really like her job but she does her job well, in order to take care of her three beautiful children- one girl and two boys. Her true passion is cosmetology. She loves to style hair and perform piercings. She made tremendous changes, and I thank God for that.

Lola is my mom's fifth child. She is the blonde of the family, literally. In my eyes, as a child, Lola was the unique one. She never liked to get dirty and loved participating in pageants. She was also very stingy and selfish, but could be super sweet at times. During middle school and high school, the Lola that we all grew up to love and support became a completely new person. She was no longer interested in pageants. She started letting her schoolwork slip. One day everybody began to notice this new girl which my sister had become. We started to ask questions like, "What's going on with you?"

She would always smile and say, "Nothing... I just don't want to do pageants anymore."

A few months later, we found out the true reason she didn't want to dress like she dressed before or keep her appearance nice like before. At the age of 15, she found out she was pregnant and waited until she was seven months pregnant to tell everybody. My mom was pissed. Everybody was mad, but we all got over it; although it took a long time. Lola gave birth to my nephew Dayron on March 24, 2007. Although being a mom was very challenging for her because she was so young, she managed to tackle all the obstacles that single moms are faced with every day. Lola has only one child, a son, who is now five years old. Although he is a crybaby, I think he is my mom's best grandchild.

Lastly are my mom's fraternal twins, Money and Tawana. They are the babies of the family. They are twins, but they are like night and day. Money is the baby boy of the bunch, and he is exactly what he is, the "baby." He began to hang with all the wrong kind of guys, and ended up getting in some trouble that cost him his freedom.

Tawana, my baby sister, is the most humble of all my mama's children. Due to the loss of her baby girl "Zye" and everyone's negative comments and judgmental actions about her being gay, she developed a certain emotional strength. Many of my family members have added to the pain and suffering that my sister is going through, because they keep badgering her about being gay. They say it's a sin, and she going to hell. Although it is a sin, being negative and judging her is not going to help her change or stop doing what she's doing. In my opinion, it's going to take prayer and time to help her. Tawana achieved her biggest goal this year, which was to get her GED and start college. We were all so proud of her; at least I know I was proud. I know my sister has a bright future and this is just the beginning for her. Tawana has endured a lot of challenges in life that made her stronger than the rest of us.

My sister Delia is my daddy's child. We were in school together for years and never knew we were sisters. Until one day, she and her cousin approached me and asked me, "What is your daddy's name." I told them "Theo," which is really his nickname. She said, "That's my daddy too." I was completely shocked. All I could say was, "Oh." I never knew I had any sisters or brothers on my daddy's side of the family. I found out I had three sisters and two brothers who I knew nothing about. It was my older sister Nikita, then me, my brother Ricky, my sister Delia, my brother Javier, and my baby sister Leah. Lord knows that man was truly busy making babies in the 80's. Although we have all met and spent some time with each other, we hardly ever see each other because my siblings on my daddy side outside of Delia and Ricky live out of town.

Even though I said I was born to both my parents doesn't mean that I was raised by them both. I never spent time with my dad as a child. I probably only saw him twice in my child. I didn't come back into contact with my daddy until the age of 21 when I had my first child.

I was raised solely by my mom, who was and still is a single mom. Outside of seeing my dad a few times in my life, I had no relationship with him, no communication, no kind of bonding, no kind of support. My family at one point was closer than anything. Nothing or no one could come between us and if they tried to; well I'll just say my family is known for kicking butts and asking questions last. I am definitely not upholding it, but the Shinns just don't take any mess from anybody I don't care what color you are: red, yellow, purple, or blue.

5 A TROUBLED FAMILY

We always had a family gathering on holidays and birthdays. I can remember our last family reunion, which was probably in 2007 or 2008; we were at Sims Scott Community Center. Everyone came home to Mississippi from different parts of America: Virginia, Texas, New York, Alabama, Georgia, Tennessee, and more. We had family reunion t-shirts that were royal blue, short sleeved, and had a big tree on the front of it with all the different family last names and background information. The weather was summery, but the breeze of the wind every few minutes gave the day a pleasant atmosphere. Those who were old enough to drink alcohol had drink. The young men and the older men in the family played football, played dominoes, and other games. The younger kids ran in the summer heat. It might have been about 80-85 degrees outside. My mom, aunts, and the rest of the women in the family were in the center kitchen preparing and cooking food for everyone to eat. The smell of the barbeque ribs, chicken, and smoked sausage, coming off the grill set the mood for the family event. The sweet smell of my aunt's pies and cakes were delightful and unforgettable. I remember thinking to myself, "This is how it's supposed to be every day." It was an awesome day. For once, it felt good to be surrounded by all of my family at one time and see everybody smiling and enjoying each other's company. One day I hope to host the biggest family reunion my family has ever seen.

Remembering everybody laughing and enjoying each other's presence doesn't make you forget the family secrets, regardless of the size of the family. Surely there are some dark secrets and a whole lot of emotional drama happening somewhere in the midst of all the cover ups, of us portraying a happy, stable, and secure family. Sometimes me and a few of my favorite girl cousins would sit back and talk like we were little old women. We were only around the age of twelve years, but we would always ask each other, "How can a family this big, be doing so badly financially? Why does our family lack doctors, lawyers, teachers, and community supporters? Why are most of the women in our family unmarried and still playing house with a man that they've been in relationships with for over five years? Why are there not any dream chasers? Why do the mothers of this family cripple the young men in this family? Why do the older men teach the younger generation of men to beat women, dog women, disrespect women, and misuse women?"

My family loves the saying, "Some things are better left unspoken." As for me, I believe that the things that are left unspoken are the things hindering this family's growth, stability, and blessings from God. Most of the females in my family were traumatized by some things that happened to them in their past; and instead of addressing the issues, they tend to think "Everythang will work itself out." I'm here to tell you, things don't work themselves out. If they did work themselves out, the things that go on behind closed doors in this family would cease to exist.

It's time for a change! It's time for someone to break the silence and I believe God chose me to be that "someone". I always heard different people tell me, "You've been here before." I'm beginning to think they're absolutely right. Many ministers and prophecies that spoke to me as a child, teenager, and now as an adult, have said "God favors you and he has a calling on your life." I'm starting to see exactly what they mean.

From the age of five until around the age thirteen or fourteen, I was molested off and on by members of my family. Not knowing how to express the pain and heartbreak that I was going through and watching the adults in my family sweep it under the rug after speaking out about it twice, I began to just keep everything to myself. Nobody understood me and they didn't even try to understand me.

"What do I mean by nobody understood me?" The adults in my family didn't do anything to stop the molestation from continuing. They didn't do anything to the guys in my family who were molesting the girls in my family. When I say girls, that's exactly what I mean. I am not the first child in this family that was molested, and I am not the last. Unlike the rest of them, I am not afraid to speak out about the molestation I endured. For some reason, I am still seeking closure for that part of my life. I know a lot of people will disagree with my decision to open my life for the whole world to see, but this is my life, that was my past, these are my tears, this is my pain, this is my struggle, and this is my story! If I can encourage just one girl or boy who is being molested or who was molested to speak out and stand up and fight back for their life, then I will feel as if I conquered life's hardest obstacle. Finding the courage to stand up to your past heartache, take back your peace of mind, change your present state, and claim your bright future in the name of Jesus!

6 LIKE IT WAS YESTERDAY

Yes! It's the weekend and my mama and aunts are getting ready to hit up their favorite club "The Green Valley;" we can't wait until they leave. Me, Ashley, and my other cousin Amy love hanging out together over my aunt Glenda's house, because we get to watch ourselves while they go out and party! From doing each other's hair and nails, to playing bakery, Lord knows we would get the worse whooping of a lifetime if we were caught with the stove turned on trying to cook a pancake in the oven. We were some crazy pre-teens growing up, but didn't know what the rest of our night had in stores for us.

After talking, eating, singing, and dancing, we began to settle down. Ashley of course was the first of us to fall asleep. We always made her get in the bed, because we are not allowed to sleep out in the open. We are girls and my mom and aunts insisted we sleep in bed together no matter what. I always wanted to know why they made sure we understood them, but tonight I will get my answer.

"Go get in the bed and stop sucking your finger, because it makes you snore louder, shoot," Stacy said.

Stacy and stayed up about twenty more minutes before I realized I was talking to myself, because Amy fell asleep too. "Get down. You bitches act like little babies!" Stacy yelled. She continued, "Amy get your ass up, because I ain't about to take you in the room and you know what mama 'nem said."

"I'on need you to take me I'ain no damn baby," Amy retorted.

"Whatever," Stacy replied.

After a few minutes, all of us were settled in bed and Amy and Ashley were already asleep. Stacy was lying on the bottom bunk pushing the top bunk mattress up and down wishing her nana would hurry up and get there. Although she loved having sleepovers with her cousins, she didn't like where her aunt lived, a trailer park that was rumored as built on top of an Indian cemetery.

Stacy was drifting off to sleep when she heard a noise that startled her. The door opened to a completely dark room, which had a night light on two minutes ago. The shut door was now open. "Wtf," Stacy said to herself. She immediately started shaking and praying that a ghost from the dead wasn't about to kill them when she noticed moving on the top bunk. At a loss for words, Stacy just laid there, eyes bugged out and body in cold sheets.

Amy was lying on the outside, Stacy lay in the middle, and Ashley was on the inside fighting to see the darkness of the room. The night sky began to send a dull gloom light through the trailer window. The shifting on the top bunk began again, only this time it didn't stop. Stacy quickly noticed a hand come from the top bunk and began rubbing on Amy. Stacy was shaking Amy and shaking Ashley, but she was unsuccessful in waking them. As the stranger on the top bunk had his way rubbing Amy's breasts, stomach, and booty Stacy knew it wouldn't be long before the hand made its way to her body. She couldn't be more on point! The hand made its way from Amy to Stacy, and she felt the wind that came as the hand moved from Amy to me.

From out of nowhere I found the courage to scream "Kel, if that's you you're going to be in big trouble! I know that's you again, and I'm telling my mama when she gets here so you better get out of here now! Leave us alone! What's wrong with you?"

I began shaking Ashley and Amy hard, "Y'all wake up, Kel in here feeling on us again! Wake up now! We got to stay awake until mama and Aunt Glenda get home!"

I would like to tell you I had a great childhood and that I always had the finer things in life, but that would be a flat-out lie! My mama worked very hard to take care of us and give us the things we needed in life, but somewhere along the way she forgot to love me the way I needed to be loved. She forgot to show me what was appropriate for a family member to do and not to do. From the age of five until I turned 13 or 14, I can't really remember which one to be exact; I was molested by some male members of my family. I was only 5 years old, how I could express what was happening to me? How could I describe my pain? I don't understand how a family member, someone who is supposed to love you and look out for you, could do some of the nasty, horrific, things they did to me. When I say they; I do mean they.

Little Stacey, five years old, no more than 50lbs, and I'm trying to fight three teenage boys off of me. It was horrible! They were touching me between my legs and kissing on breasts I didn't even have.

I hated them. I hated my mama. I hated my auntie. I hated everybody in my family for so long until, I hated myself! I still suffer from nightmares and flashbacks from my past.

I hated being skinny! I hated hearing family and friends say "You're so boney." That one little statement pissed me off; just like a fat person hates to be called Fat. I hated to be called Skinny. I thought about getting the Botox injection and breast implants. Why am I so unhappy with myself? Maybe it's because I've been told too many times that I'm too skinny, too poor, and too thin. I'm tired of hearing I need to eat more.

What is wrong with me? Maybe I critique myself too much. I don't know. I need to make some changes, because I'm not happy with myself. When I look in the mirror, I see a girl that was to be full of life, with dreams bigger than the world she lives in. She had tons of confidence, determination, charisma, and a great sense of humor! My grandma, mama, and aunts always said, "I swear that gal been here before."

Having no daddy to cry out to, no daddy to tell I was hurt beyond measures by my cousins; I was left to grow up this bitter, scared to love little girl. I can only recall seeing my daddy two times out of my childhood. The last time I saw him as a child, he told me he would buy me a bike for my birthday. That was 18 birthdays ago. For a long time, I hated that man. I told myself that I would never forgive him for disowning me and leaving me to learn how I should be treated by a man on my own.

7 SAVING MY OWN LIFE

Everybody thought me and Tavarus would be together forever but after about the third year of our relationship, I began to question that "forever" thought. We rented our own place in January 2005. When I repeat the saying, "You don't know a person until you move in with them," it is not a lie. Slowly but surely I began to see the man I loved, my soon to be husband, turn into a man I feared and hated. No one knows what goes through the mind of a woman who has lived through many years of physical, emotional, and mental abuse from a man she thought loved her. I have been out of that relationship for three years now and I still have nightmares and flashbacks. I wake up in cold sweats and deal with emotional defects with myself due to the hands of my abuser. I'm 26 years old now, the single mother of three beautiful children. Yes, I'm still single!

Sometimes, I don't know whether I'm going or coming. My family life has a tremendous effect on me. I just don't understand how a family so big be doing so bad, struggling, hiding behind family secrets, and lies. What is it? What must I do to change things for the good of my family; most of all, for me and my children.

I hurt badly at times. I don't really like listening to moody music, because I become a train wreck of emotions. I feel like I watched my life pass me by. I deserve so much more and I expected so much more. How can I regain the strength, ambition, determination, and motivation that I had as a child and teenager? I want my life back! I want to be married in a healthy, happy, stable relationship with a real man who loves me for me; a man who is God fearing, honest, charming, loving, caring, stable, family oriented, and so many other characteristics. I feel like my husband has passed me by; like I already had him, but I let him go. Is it true that God will send you a husband, and if you let him go you may never get another chance? Lord please don't let this be true! I know I'm capable of being a good strong wife. I'm so tired of all these lonely nights, and tired of crying with no one to comfort me. I'm just tired of being tired.

I've been at my grandma's house for two days now; me and my brats. I don't understand why I'm so lazy when it comes to handling important things; I've been procrastinating on finishing up my cd, schoolwork, and writing this darn book! I really must get it together. My mind is just so cluttered with other, distracting thoughts. I'm so tired of struggling and wondering where my next meal will come from.

Every day I wake up, I am praying for a miracle from somewhere. If it wasn't for my faith, I wouldn't have anything! I have a show tomorrow night at the Holiday Inn. Lord knows I'm praying that I get signed or something; I'm patiently waiting for my chance to become the star that lives inside of me.

Trying to reach and achieve your dreams while being a single mom definitely is a lot of work. I'm on the road to happiness within myself. I pray that God never allows me to become abuse bait for another man, as long as I'm on this earth. When it comes to my kids and their dads, it's kind of hard for me to express what I'm feeling in my heart. Yes, I want my kid's dads to be in their life, Yes, I want my kids to love and cherish their dads as much as they love and cherish me. Yes, I sometimes wish I had chosen other fathers for my children, but let's be real. In all honesty, I love my kids daddies equally because, they both gave me the best thing any woman could ask for; smart, beautiful, and healthy children."

When I say I have some beautiful kids that's exactly what I mean! My oldest daughter Justice, who is the reason for the season, she was my first. She made me grow up. She made me want better for her and myself. She is such a little lady; and she has the longest prettiest black hair a five year old should have. She is so helpful and so smart. She encourages me, and boy does she love her momma. She is my "Little Cheerleader/Cover-girl Model."

Then there's my love, my heart, my lifeline who happens to be my second born child, my son Demarri. He is mommy's everything! Demarri is what I'd like to call a "Complete country boy." He loves to do everything that a boy supposed to do and more. He loves sports, doing yard work, fixing cars, cleaning, playing the drums, and so much more. I love my son. Yes, I do!

Last but definitely not least is my baby; my mini me, Jewel. I like to refer to her as "Jewel Chanel." My baby is so adorable! She has the prettiest big brown eyes, the brightest smile, and boy does she love to sing!

It's kind of ironic that I'm sitting here in my room thinking back to when I first found out I was pregnant with Jewel and all I could do was cry. I felt so low, so bad. I had just called it quits with Tavarus and went back home to Mississippi for good.

I moved to Country Air Apartments in Columbus, Mississippi. I have always been the kind of person who stayed to herself when living in an apartment complex, not knowing what I was about to face. I worked two jobs, Ryan's and McDonald's. I was a workaholic and I was still in school, tell me I am not bad. It's funny the way God place people into your life unexpectedly and allow them to change your whole perspective on life.

After me and Tavarus had our last big fight, the one where he pulled a knife on me and put it to my throat in front of our child, I knew then that I had to let this piece of a relationship go for good. I knew, either he was going to me or I was going to kill him. I was so terrified. That night, I thought my life was over. I can remember looking into his eyes and thinking, "He really hates me, and he's going to do it. He's going to kill me this time for real." My daughter Justice was just sitting there she was only 2 at the time. My face filled with tears as I begged him not to do it. I was saying everything I thought he wanted to hear like; "I love you, I'm sorry, I'll do whatever you ask me to. Please, please don't kill me. I'm sorry Tavarus. I'm sorry." Those horrific cries went unheard by all of the people who live in my apartment complex, strange right? He pushed me to the floor and went into the kitchen to put away the knife. I just lay there on the floor crying out to God and begging him to get me out of that situation for the last time. God heard my cry. He answered my prayer. The very next day I called my uncle and my brothers and I told them I wanted Tavarus gone. I wanted him gone that day. I told them what happened and everybody was so pissed off they wanted to kill him. Instead of killing him, my uncle bought him a bus ticket and sent his ass back to his home town Detroit. My next door neighbors and I quickly became cool due to the facts that I had two kids and they had plenty of children for my kids to play with.

8 DEAD BEAT DADS

They all should be executed! Of course I don't mean that. It's just a thought I had in the past. Forget them, it's their loss because my babies were my best creation and I don't regret them for anything! I do regret who I chose to father my children. It is so hard to really wrap my mind around the thought of raising my kids alone, without any kind of support from their fathers for the rest of my life. I mean what kind of man can really go to sleep or go an entire day without even considering contacting his child or children? I really hate to say this, but trying to convince myself that I don't hate my kids' fathers is like trying to convince the world that Jesus didn't die on the cross for our sins!

My kid's daddies must be the most selfish, ignorant, uncaring, irresponsible men on the planet! They never even attempt to see how their kids are doing. They don't even know if they are alive. It's just pathetic as hell!

No one else can bring you out of the storms and tests of life only God can.

I thought I found my soul mate. I thought the wait was over, but I was in for a rude awakening. You broke me down mentally socially and physically. I don't think I ever fought so much in my life, but that man was so controlling and evil and so sneaky with it. He had everybody in my family fooled. They thought I was the one starting all the bull and chaos. They were still in my life, but they were still wrong. The only thing that messed me up the most, he did everything I asked of him. He would kill for me, but he had the other side of him that I did not see often. I was about to be introduced to it sooner than later.

He would never hit me in the face, bloody my nose, or leave any revealing bruises that people might notice. He would leave marks on my legs, arms, and back! Anything could tick him off! In seconds he could go from being calm and relaxing, to a full blown rage. The abuse had gotten to the point that I could feel his eyes going up and down my head, if I said the wrong thing or spoke to guys when we were out in public. I had become so familiar to fighting with him or should I say with him jumping on me all the time, that all I could say was, "Tavarus I'm sorry" and cry until I could no longer cry anymore! I can remember when he use to smack me in front of our friends and sometimes family. Nobody would ever help me. They would let him dog walk me!

After each fight I would lie in bed and ask myself the same questions; "Why am I still with him? Why am I too afraid to leave him? Although he hurt me, I love him beyond all of the pain he caused me. Is something wrong with that?" He didn't like my friends so I couldn't hang out with any of them.

I always thought we had a bright future together. I thought we would never part, but after about six years of physical and verbal abuse, I called it quits. "Why, Tavarus? Why? I loved you with everything I had, and you took everything in me."

On so many occasions I tried to contact Tavarus to get help with our kids. He hasn't had or kept a job since I left him, until now. I always tried to contact him before their birthdays and the holidays to see if he wanted me to come and pick him up so he can spend time with the kids. He would always say no, because his girlfriend wasn't welcome. After constantly being rejected, all his lies and broken promises to the kids, I just completely stopped communication. I cut him off completely; no calls, no texts, and no social network communication. There is no reason a mother should have to run behind the father to ask for help with his children. He knows what he helped create.

I met Chanel's father in the summer of 2009. We lived next door from each other. He is three years younger than I am. Trust me when I say, that's exactly how I treated him. Our relationship happened so fast! It was like, one minute we were just friends and the next minute he's head over hills in love with me.

It scared me; the fact that a man could love me so fast and be so serious and sincere with it. I was so mean to him, because I was honestly still in the process of getting over Tavarus. We were only separated a month. I know to some people think that's a "trashy" move, but everybody makes mistakes and not everybody falls in love the same way. I got pregnant by Monte the second time we had sex. Until this day, I don't comprehend how or I just refuse to comprehend how it happened.

Monte is a caramel skin tone, kind of on the short side, and has the best skin complexion I've ever seen! He was always very respectful to me. He never called me out of my name, at least not to my face. He treated me like a queen, but I treated him like garbage. Why did I treat him badly? I wasn't accustomed to a man treating me right and treating me with respect.

Monte joined the military while we were together, and he left for Basic Training when I was around five months pregnant with our daughter. I broke up with him before he left for Basic Training. He wanted me to marry him and I said, "No, I'm not ready". Although, some people said I was stupid for not marrying him and hanging on to his military coat tail, that's just not me. I have never been that type of female. I was still at a point in my life where I was still trying to love myself, so how could I jump in a marriage with all the extra emotional baggage I had going on in me?

I went to visit Monte occasionally while he was in Basic Training. After I had Chanel in March 2010, I waited until she was eleven days old and I took her to see him in Augusta, Georgia. You would think he would be sitting in the motel room patiently waiting, right? Wrong! When I got there he was still on the base and called to tell me he would see her in the morning, because was too drunk! I said, "I bet you a lie, you better get your ass here within an hour."

When he finally showed up, he was indeed drunk. I was completely pissed! He looked at her and said, "Hey, daddy baby." He then lay on the bed and fell asleep. The very next morning I got up, got dressed, and my cousins and I left him and Chanel at the room and went shopping. Although he was drunk the first time he saw her, he made it his duty to spend the rest of our vacation with her. I wouldn't exactly say I have a problem with Monte; I would just like to say that I am completely disappointed in the father he allowed himself to become.

He requested a blood test for Chanel, which he went behind my back to get. It came back 99.98% that she is his child. Even after finding out the results, he made no effort to add her to his Military insurance and benefits. He would lie constantly about sending money, clothes, birthday boxes, and Christmas boxes to her. It got to the point where I just said forget this and I started contacting lawyers and his military commander to see if I could get some help from him for Chanel.

Then he decided to meet an old woman, have a baby by her, and marry her all in one year. Still, he gave me no support for Chanel. I did what any other mother would do; I cut him off completely; no communication of any kind! I did everything I could to make him suffer, because I know deep down inside it was killing him not to know the well-being of his child, and not to know what I was doing. Yes, I allowed him to bring out the evil, sneaky, investigating side of me. Like the saying goes, "The people you try to hurt the most are the ones you love the most," and only God knows how much I loved Monte.

But in the words of Tupac, "Life Goes On," and I've moved on.

9 DAILY THOUGHTS

As a child, I loved to write poetry, short stories, and plays. But as I got older, I transformed my writings into "Daily Thoughts". My daily thoughts are honest and unrestrained; I write whatever is on my mind and heart at that current moment. I will share some of my past daily thoughts with you; that way you can see how different my mind frame has changed over the years.

I need to get my butt back in church. When I'm not in church, I'm lost completely.

Daily Thought: (12/24/2009) "This morning I opened my eyes, but tonight was when I really woke up. I know that may seem confusing to you, but it is very understandable. When I opened my eyes this morning, I opened them with fear, wonders, heartache, and pain. During this entire year I walked around with my eyes open for the world to see, but closed and hidden from the real person who is me. I never thought the day would come when my life seemed better off without me. My emotions are conflicting, my heart is raging, my mind is stuck inside of a molasses jar and my feet are implanted in cement.

Why must love hurt? That is a question I have asked myself and others many times. I have been in and out of love to the point that I feel as if I don't deserve to love or to be loved. Why do I feel that way? Why don't I deserve the compassion, comfort, support, and sexual pleasure that being in love has to offer? Maybe it's because I have taken love for granted on so many occasions, or maybe it's because love has taken me for granted."

Part 2 - "When the New Year comes in, where will I be? What will I be doing? Who will I be with? Most of all, who will I be? Most questions I can't answer today or tomorrow. One question I can answer is, "who will I be?" I hope to become a better woman, mom, daughter, and friend. I mostly hope to have the courage to become a better lover when the time permits. I will regenerate the power that I once had, but have now lost. I will take control of my life, my future, and my happiness! No one will determine my future but the Lord, and only He can change and direct my footsteps. I will be the best mom I can be, the best friend I can be, and the soon to be best companion. I am my own shadow. I am my own hinderer. I am the one person who is holding me back from future happiness. No longer will I stop myself from future success.

I'm not sure if heartache is considered "pressure" but, in my current situation it has built up more pressure on my mind, body, and soul than anything has ever done before. Looking out to all my family smiling and happy when I'm dying inside, trying so hard to hold back this ocean of tears behind my eyes...

How could he? This pain is unbearable. Thinking there was still a chance for us, he proved me wrong by getting married. What do I do with the love? Where do I go from here? I'm not going to even fake like I just don't care or I'm not hurt because, I wouldn't be keeping it 100% with myself or you! It really hurts like hell. I guess that's what my ass gets for snooping on Facebook, but it's cool. I'm going to laugh it off, because that piece of a marriage won't last six months! He isn't anything but a cheating, manipulating, conniving, lying ass man! I wonder what his Momma got to say about this. She probably said "We all got to make our own mistakes." She loves to say that. I haven't heard from my first deadbeat baby daddy in a long time. I wonder what he doing? Probably, somewhere lying and thinking about me. Hell, both of them are probably thinking about me. I'm the truth!

I wish these birds would shut the hell up! What are they so happy about anyways? I swear Jewel calls my name for fun. "Ma, Ma, Ma" that's all she knows but, I guess I can't blame her she doesn't have a father figure in her life. Her dad is in the Army and she probably sees him twice a year. Other than that, he doesn't communicate with her at all. From the looks of things she doesn't even exist to him the rest of the year. I bet that drag queen hears from him every day. "Deadbeats I tell ya!" They all should be shot in the head execution style.

Between working on my upcoming cd, going to school, writing this book, and lastly being a single mother, I barely have a second to think of myself, but I won't complain. Things could definitely be worse."

"Some nights I just sit up and stare at my kids while they sleep so peaceful, without a care in the world. Not knowing mommy is breaking down in the inside because, I'm alone raising them and I feel like I'm not providing them with everything they need and want. But I'm doing the best I can that I know! I just continue to pray and keep my faith in the Lord because; I know he won't put no more on me than I can bear. I want to be remembered for my good works in my community and country."

He destroyed me! I still find myself waking up in the middle of the nights with cold sweats from having nightmares of the abuse Tavarus put me through. Although, he still denies the fact that he abused me, God knows the truth. I just don't know how to move on from this, how can I get my heart over this pain, how can I ever love or trust another man again? I'm so lost in my emotions, Lord please help me to get over my past heartache and pain. Although I've had my share of pain and heartache, I know that God has not forgotten me or left me. Things happen in life that we can't control or foresee. We just have to continue to live each day according to the word of the Lord.

10 A TROUBLED PAST

Although it may seem like I caught hell all my life, at different points of my life, I was dishing it out. I must be honest, as a teenager I gave my momma pure the hell. In the past, I hung out with my cousins a lot. Some of them are older than I am, some are younger, but we all got together and stole clothes, shoes, etc., from the mall. Most of my cousins really needed the things they stole, but me… I didn't need a thing. My momma made sure I was dress in the best clothes and shoes every day. To this day I still can't give my mom a reasonable answer for why I began to steal.

I would tell her, "Because you wouldn't get it for me; or I didn't have the money." It was a flat-out lie. My mama didn't send us anywhere broke. If I wanted something, even if I couldn't get it that day, I knew that she would make sure I got it soon. Stealing for me became a hobby. It was fun. It was like I was getting away with doing something bad and getting to keep my money at the same time.

How many of you know that if you steal, you will get caught? It might not be that day, but you will get caught one day. That day finally came for me. I got caught stealing out of Wal-Mart in Georgia. The dumbest part about it, I was stealing a shirt for somebody else and had a purse full of money, because I was also working at McDonalds.

I was 17 years old when my momma found out that I and my friends were stealing out of stores. Lucky for me, the day we got caught stealing in the Mall, I didn't steal a thing. I said to them, "I'll take y'all to the Mall, but I'm not stealing no more, because I gotta graduate and I'm not trying to go to jail with y'all". Sure enough, one of my friends got caught trying to steal from the store in the mall owned by the Chinese people. She stole some black Dickies pants. I left the store after browsing, because I could feel it in my stomach that she was about to get caught that day, and she did. They acted like she robbed the store. All of the security guards started running toward us and hollering, "Who got the pants? Who got them?"

I started crying and yelling, "It wasn't me. I didn't steal anything. It wasn't me!" Since my friend wouldn't own up to stealing the pants, they took all us into the mall's Security Room where they interrogated us and screamed at us for about twenty minute. By then the mall manager was fed up and said, "Everybody is going to jail if somebody doesn't tell me who stole those pants. Y'all got five minutes!" I looked at my other two friends who were looking at me. Then we all began to look at the friend who had stolen the pants, but was refusing to say a word. I gave the manager my purse.

I said, "Here, you can check my purse and search me. I didn't do it!"

I know it wasn't anybody, but God who got me out of that situation. About five minutes later, the man that owned the Chinese store came walking into the security room. He looked dead at the mall manager and said, "I saw her, she did not steal from my store. She left when the others were in the dressing room. She was no trouble, but she has a bad group of friends."

I started crying again, because here I was at the prime of my life. My graduation was only a few weeks away. I'm up here in a security room, minutes from jail! I'm a good talker; I always have been a good talker, probably always will be a good talker. I started to talk to the mall manager. I started by saying, "I apologize for my behavior, and my friends behavior. But I am not the girl you think of me. I have a momma that's probably going to kill me when she finds out about this. And I have a job in which I love and they love me. I will be graduating from high school in a few weeks. I don't know why I tend to hang with people that don't mean me no good; but I promise you this, if you let me go, you'll never see or hear about me stealing no more."

When I tell you God was moving in my favor he said, "All you girls give me a phone number to contact your parents or whoever your guardian is." I was the first to offer my home phone number, but the others were reluctant to tell him.

He asked them for the phone numbers again and one of my friends said, "I don't have any parents. I live wherever I can."

Then the other friend said, "I am here from out of town. My momma doesn't even nowhere I am and she probably doesn't care"

Lastly, my other friend started whimpering with tears in her eyes, hung her head even lower and whispered, "My mom is dead, and my dad doesn't want anything to do with me."

At that moment, I began to weep with all my friends, because here I am thinking my life is so messed up, that my family is so screwed up, but these girls that I knew to be my friends had no family at all. The mall manager looked as if he could just go into his office and breakdown. It was like he was thinking, "One of these girls could have been my daughter."

Between all the crying and everybody expressing their self, who comes running into the office like somebody had died? Nobody but my mama. She looked so ashamed and hurt by my actions. She started talking to the manager and telling him how I wasn't raised like this; some of the same stuff I already told him. He seemed to find comfort in the fact that my Mom came to my rescue and she seemed so scared for my well-being and reputation. He spoke with her for a few more minutes, and then he lit in on my tail.

He said, "You have a mother that is concerned about you, that loves you, and you're hanging out with these girls whom you have no compatibility with and break her heart. You should be ashamed. You better be glad your mama came on, because you would have been heading to the same place your friends are; to jail!" My mouth dropped. I was thinking, "What happened to the nice man he was twenty minutes ago?" Although he hurt my feelings, I knew he still had a job to do. I was just grateful that I had my momma, and that she came to my rescue.

It wasn't a month after my graduation when I was caught stealing from Wal-Mart. This time, I went to jail. No amount of tears could save me; not even my momma's tears. Like I said before, I don't know what made me go in that store and steal that shirt, when I knew it wasn't even for me. I learned a valuable lesson that day and a more valuable lesson on my court date. When the judge said, "You are here by sentenced to 45 days in the county jail," all I could do was look back at my mama and start crying. She was crying already. It was like she knew I was about to be taken away from her. It hurt me so bad to see the shame, pain, and fear in my mom's eyes. I made a promise to myself and my momma. When I got out of that trouble, I was gone do right; and I did.

I completed those 45 days and ran home. I didn't wait on my mom to pick me up or anything. I ran all the way home, because we only lived ten minutes away from the jail. When I made it home, nobody was there, but the key was still under the mat. I began to smile even harder, when I looked out in the parking lot and saw that my car was parked and needed to be washed. I was so glad my momma didn't take my car away from me. When they came home, I was hiding in the closet to surprise them. You know I have a lot of sisters and brothers, so they came in the house all extra loud and stuff. I waited until they walked by the front room closet door and then I busted out the closet and said, "SURPRISE, HONEY I'M HOME."

Everybody started jumping and hollering all around me. My mama walked in from checking the mailbox and said, "Why the hell y'all hollering in my house." Then she saw the reason, me. It was like a weight was immediately lifted up from her body. She ran and gave me a hug. She also told me that I'd put on some weight. The next day, my mom took me shopping, to lunch, and to talk to my manager about my job. My manager was so happy to see me.

He said, "Don't you get your butt in no more trouble, and be at work tomorrow"

At that moment I just looked up to the sky and said, "Thank you God for yet another blessing." To have my freedom, family, and job back, I knew at that very moment nothing in this world was worth losing. I haven't stolen anything since the day I went to jail, and I don't plan to ever steal anything. Nothing is worth losing my FREEDOM! Always remember that, "Trouble is easy to get into, but it's hard to get out of."

11 BLACK ANGEL

No words can express the pain I feel right now. I'm lost. My heart is dying. My eyes are in pain from all the tears that's flowing out of them. I lost a part of me, my family, my life, my heart, my niece. Zycheria is gone, the Lord called her home September 20, 2010. Where do I go from here? How can I be strong for my sister, when I'm in so much pain myself? My niece was just like my own child, so the pain I'm feeling is unbearable. I know you're not supposed to ask God why, but I would really like to know the reason my niece was lifted from our life at such an early age. At the age of six months, her life had just begun, and it ended before she could even crawl, walk, talk, ride her bike, say "Mama" or "Daddy." Oh God how my heart cries out for your comfort. I still remember this day like it was yesterday, and it's been almost two years since I lost my niece. I remember feeling this way and just wondering, "Why?" We all know God makes no mistakes and everything he does is for the best.

On March 2, 2010, my sister and I gave birth to our baby girls at almost the same time. They were about three hours apart. They both were born healthy and beautiful. We titled them "twin cousins." They were always dressed alike. They had the same strollers and car seats. We had two of everything, not expecting the day would come when they would be separated from each other's side.

My niece came down with meningitis and suffered a massive shutdown throughout her body. The pain was unbearable and the tears were unstoppable. Completely grief struck, I didn't know how to be strong for my sister. Zycheria was her first and only child. On top of that my sister is happily gay, but certain situations and crisis in our family life caused her to interact with the male gender. In the end, she found out about my niece and was overly scared, excited, and grateful to God for her unexpected but patiently awaited baby girl.

12 BEGINNING AGAIN

From looking at me and listening to me speak; you would not know that I and my kids became homeless three weeks before my book was expected to come out. Out of all the things I've been through in life and out of all the things I overcame, who knew that my one biggest fears would come true; having to pack up and leave my mama's house over a trivial issue and moving into a motel with my kids. I heard them constantly ask, "Mama, why we got to stay here? Why we can't stay at grandma's house with everybody else? Where we gone live? How we gone take a bath?" Those questions alone broke me down inside, because I had no answer for my kids. I had no idea how I was going to swing getting an apartment and still catch up on my car note. Only working twenty-five hours a week with no other income, I knew it was impossible.

I tried to locate a homeless shelter and contacted a few family members. I went to the police station and signed up for that assistance program. Then I said, "Forget it. These are my kids and I'm responsible for their safety and security."

So, I started searching online for an apartment. With all the apartment prices so high, plus the deposit, I knew that only God would bring me through that situation. At first I was upset but, then I just looked to the sky and remembered the promise God made to me- which he will never leave, nor forsake me. I said "God, yet will I trust in you. I know this is just a test of my faith, and I will keep holding on to your unchanging hands."

It was so hard trying not to worry when my babies are looking at me as if they were trying to read through me. At one point, I hated myself. I thought that I was ugly and all kinds of other degrading things. My self-esteem was completely gone. For so many years I just let go of all my dreams and goals until finally I said, "Enough is enough. I'm tired of living like this and feeling like this." I started going back to church and became more active in my church. It was like, slowly but surely God was taking bits of pieces of my life that were scattered and began putting them back together one by one. It's amazing; when you really and truly let go and let God have his way, you see the immediate effect on your life!

I recently started the Rising Stars Youth Program in my community. It helps girls, between the ages of eight and 17 who are at higher risk of becoming a victim of child molestation, fatherless homes, single parent homes, teen pregnancy, low self-esteem, or school drop outs! I truly believe that God put this program in my vision for a reason. Our community and state is so small, but has the highest rates on just about everything in the negative youth statistic areas. Someone has to say, "Ok! That's it! I'm willing to sacrifice my time and devote it to uplifting and reconstructing the foundation of our youth. I do believe God handpicked me to be that someone!"

In life you go through up and downs. You experience changes, good and bad. You encounter trials and tribulations; but you just have to remember to hold on to God's promise to you, and get out there and seek your inheritance. What God has for you, it is for you! No matter what your mother, father, sister, brother, or any family, friends, or community officials say, you can make it and overcome the negative statistics. BUT only if you try!

I just would like to take this time and thank everyone who has helped and supported me on this journey of finding that lost little girl from my past. The grace of God directed her to the woman I am today! I am a leader! I am a victim of child molestation. I am a fatherless girl. I am a victim of a single family home. I am a victim of domestic violence.

I am now a single mother of three beautiful children! No matter what anyone says I AM A SURVIVOR!

I'm finally at a point in my life where I can honestly say I am at peace with myself and my past. I have truly forgiven everyone that hurt or affected me in the past. You can't control the cards you are dealt in life you just have to be willing to play the game until the end. Win or lose you can always start over! Never give up on your dreams and goals, because they really do come true. I no longer have those nightmares. I no longer dwell on the things from my past. I have let go and let God. When I say "My God can move mountains," that's exactly what I mean! I just look back over my life and I cry, because no matter how hard I tried to pull away from God, he never let me go! He kept me when I didn't want to be kept. I just thank and praise him for never leaving or forsaking me. God's love for me saved me from drowning in my past sorrows.

All I want to do is raise my kids to the best of my ability and insure that their future is as bright as the sun. They are truly the reason why I never really threw in the towel on my dreams. I knew that someone had to break the cycle for my family, and I believe God handpicked me to be that someone who does just that for my family. You will go through trials and tribulations, you will have good and bad days but you must never let go of God unchanging hands because he is the only way. No one else can bring you out of the storms and tests of life. Only God can...

13 FROM A MOTHERS PERSPECTIVE

When I found out I was pregnant with my daughter Stacey Shuntel Shinn, I was seventeen years old in high school a junior playing on the basketball team for Hamilton High School. I must say I was doing pretty well despite of the poverty stricken living situation. I was desperate to accomplish my goals in life, which was to be a basketball player and a nurse. After I found out that I was pregnant with Stacey, like any other responsible mother, I had to put all my dreams on hold to handle the responsibility of raising my child. I didn't raise her on my own. My mom, dad, sisters, and brothers helped me. Also, the man I thought was Stacey's father, the love of my life throughout my high school years; James porter took his place as her father. He was so ready to take charge of his fatherly duties.

I know James was going be a great dad, but the rumors soon started to float around about "Stacey "not being his child. I began to look at her very careful one day and came to the conclusion that the rumor perhaps might be right. I questioned myself, "How could I have let this happen? How could it be? When and how was I going to tell the man I was so in love with, that the daughter he loved so much was not his?" Oh my how I cried, I cried. I was so angry and emotional with myself. How could I have known that I could get pregnant after having sex with someone once? I thought we were being careful. Sometimes I wondered if he purposely got me pregnant. He was more sexually active then I was, and he was older than me. I only had sex with him twice the first night. One thing lead to another and we got very sexually passionate. The next evening we talked about the night before. I think he asked me to have sex with him again.

I said, "No, I don't think I better." I told him I only did it because I was mad at my boyfriend James. I was told by a close friend of mine that he was with this other girl, so I just wanted to get even.

He said, "Oh he's with her right now, I just seen them at the store together." Of course I got angry and furious real quick. I started crying and he held me and walked me to my sister's trailer. It happened again we had sex! Damn, I was young, dumb, and stupid. I got played! I never once thought that I would get pregnant by this guy! Plus, it only happened twice.

On the other hand James and I were having unprotected sex at the time, but I didn't care if I had gotten pregnant by him. I wanted to be with him forever. So, I built up the courage to call and tell James that the baby might not be his. The phone rang and he answered, "Hello."

I said, "We need to talk about the baby."

He thought something was wrong with Stacey, but I told him that she is okay, but we still needed to talk. He refused to wait for me to tell him. He wanted to know right then, but I didn't want to tell him over the phone.

I finally broke down crying, and he kept asking, "What's wrong? What is it? Tell me if you are okay...is the baby ok?"

I stopped crying long enough to tell him in a light voice, "She's not yours. You're not the father."

There was an immediate silence and a long pause over the phone. He started crying with me and saying, "I don't believe you. How did you let this happen?"

I explained to him what I did, why I did it, and who I did it with. He then began to tell me that he wasn't messing around with her; he was only giving her and another lady a ride to the store. She liked him, but he was in love with me and didn't cheat on me. I cried even harder. I thought my whole world was coming to an end. I felt so betrayed my friends that told me the lie in the first place. I hung up the phone with James. Back then we had to use the pay phones. I hung up the phone and walked back to my sister's trailer crying my eyes and heart out, sniffling all the way there. It took me about fifteen minutes to make it back to the trailer park. Because of all the tears in my eyes, I could hardly see where I was going.

By the time I made it in the trailer park, James was in his car, flying and swerving out of control. My first thought was "Oh my god, he's about to kill me." He was actually coming to take her away from me.

I asked, "Him what you are doing?"

He said "She's mine and I'm taking her with me."

I said, "No, she's not. She's not yours give her back! You've been drinking and you're driving crazy!"

He yelled "Do you think I'm going to hurt my own damn baby? She is mines and I'm taking her."

I started yelling "I'm going to call the police and your mom on you." No matter what I said, he didn't care. He refused to listen. After several minutes, my sisters and a friend of hers convinced him to leave "Stacey" and wait until the next day to get things cleaned up and get sober. He kissed her on the forehead and said, "Daddy loves you".

He looked at me and said, "I can't believe this. Why did you do this to me? I thought you said you loved me."

I was still crying and yelling to him, "I do, I do love you. I'm sorry. I'm so sorry. I didn't mean for this to happen."

The downside of this situation was that, I had to tell the guy named "Sebo," that he was my baby's father.

His response was, "How is that when you've been with James all the time?" He also said that she wasn't his child and some other things.

I went on to tell him, "I feel the same way you do, how could this happen. I don't want you to be the father of my child." I wanted James to be the father, but that was impossible. We both knew it, because "Stacey" had all of his features. How can I overlook that? How could he overlook it?

He repeatedly insisted that she was not his child, so I had no choice but to go to the child support office. He refused to do anything for her. By the time she turned five years old, he wanted to try and claim her on his taxes. He promised her he was going to buy her clothes and a bike." Oh yea, he gave her $5.00 in five years?! She was glad to have the money, so I didn't want to make a big deal out of the situation in front of her; but oh how I wanted to cut up! "Five dollars, you give my baby five dollars?" He hasn't done anything for her since she's been on earth. The names I called him... I refuse to recall. If you're a mom in my shoes, you know the words I called him.

When she turned thirteen, I finally started receiving child support for her. He eventually stopped paying, and the lady at the child support office said something about him not being employed at the time. So, I contacted "Support Kids" They found him and we started receiving child support payments once we relocated to Georgia.

My main point is how Stacey became the young lady she is today. She started out at the daycare along with her cousins. From there, she went to Head Start where she immediately made friends and became a teacher's pet. She was very outgoing and outspoken. Some people say she has an "Old soul" and that "She's been here before." Her first day of Head Start was very hard for the both of us. She was ready and all excited the day before, and I was ready and excited for her as well. The next morning came, and I got her up and got her dressed. I told her, "Hurry up. Here comes your bus." She stopped dead in her tracks and looked at me like, "What bus...you're not going?" I went ahead and answered her unspoken question, "No, I'm not going".

She started saying, "I don't want to go on that bus momma. Please don't let me get on that bus. I don't want to go. No mama..."

She was crying at the top of her lungs and pulling on my clothes as terrified as can be. My heart just dropped. I thought I was doing her so wrong, so I told the bus patrol lady that I would take her to school in my car.

She stop me and said, "I know it's hard to let them go, but she is gone be alright. We go through this all the time with the kids and their parents. She told me to give Stacey to her and walk away. I hesitated. My eyes were tearing up. I took a deep breath and let her hand go from mine and gave her to the bus patrol lady and walked away. As I walked away, I cried the whole way to the house. I can still hear her yelling on the bus "Mama, mama". I just broke down. I called the school and told the principal that I was coming to pick her up, but she said, "Why, she is laughing and playing now. She is okay now. Let her finish up the rest of the day."

Sure enough, she jumped off the bus laughing, talking, and waving bye to her new found friends as if this morning never happened. It was such a relief off my heart to know she did have a good day at school and made friends. The next day she got on the bus with no problems. I said "Thank you God. It's going to be okay."

Well, Stacey was familiar with the kids and it was graduation time for the Head Start. Of course, you know what that means... Now I have to get her ready for a new school, new kids, and new teachers. Kindergarten time! I took her to school sign her up, and she was too happy go lucky. She was playing with the kids and talking to her teacher, until she realized she had to stay there the rest of the day. In the classroom, she flipped completely out. She started crying and screaming, "Mama don't leave me, please mama I'll be good. Don't leave me here please." Once again, my heart dropped, and I had tears in my eyes. I hung my head down and said, "I can't do this. I can't leave her here. She's not ready yet." I told her teachers I would bring her back the next day. They said, "If she stays, she'll get used to it. She going to cry a while, but she will stop when you leave." Well, I wasn't so sure of that. I mean, I didn't know if they would hit her, pinch her, and slap her or something to scare her into being quiet. My, my, my... That was a tough decision once again, but I left her there.

I left Stacey in the school with those strangers. I couldn't even drive when I got in the car. I think I was crying worse than she was crying. It was so hard, because she was my first child. So, everything was new to her and new to me. Well, the teachers said she'd adapt and she did! She came home telling me about all her friends and how nice her teachers were to her. I said once again, "Thank you God! I am not such a bad mom after all." I did what I thought was right, and I'm just glad that it turned out fine for her.

So, Stacey graduated from kindergarten, and it was time for the first grade. Only this time, she has her friends she already know from kindergarten. She walked in like a big girl and told me, "I'm not gone cry. You can go ahead." I smiled and said, "Okay," and went home.

I drove home, cleaned up, and waited for Stacey to get out of school and tell me about her day. She gained more friends, and this became ongoing throughout all her school years, all the way up to her high school graduation. She tried out for cheerleading when she was at Caledonia Middle School, but she didn't make the team. I moved to west point which was closer to my job. It also meant she had to relocate to another school in West Point.

Stacey tried out for the cheerleading team there. After tryouts she came home looking sad like she didn't make the team and shouted, "I made it!" Everyone in the house started clapping and yelling, "Yea! You did it. I knew you could do it." She also became a part of the school choir. She tried out for band, playing the flute, and she made that too. She was also competed again her class in the spelling bee contest and won a chance to go on to the next round, where she would compete against other schools. She didn't win but, she was okay with her accomplishment. She said she didn't want to do it again anyway.

It was moving time again! I had to move to Columbus, because I was behind on the rent. I found a nice home in the East Columbus area. It was a very lovely home. I stayed their awhile and enrolled the kids into the Columbus schools. This is when Stacey and her brother Rico started getting in trouble. Rico was going to protect her whether she was right or wrong. She would tell him if someone was picking on her and he'd beat them up. He wasn't alone when it came to protecting her. All of her cousins were behind him. She was the smallest of them all, very tiny, but had the most demanding voice ever. She would even scare them to do what she said. They would always tell her that they were tired of fighting for her and that she would have to start fighting for herself. She would always tell them that she didn't know how to fight, but one day she had no choice but to fight.

Some girls at school approached her and tried to jump her. She held her own, but was conquered. You best believe that fight wasn't over. It had just begun. Once her cousins and brothers found out, they found those same girls, beat the snot out of them, and dared them to ever touch her again.

During all of that, she met this little boy. She had a crush on him and he had one on her as well. He lived about three houses down the street from us. As soon as they got acquainted, I moved them again. Only this time, we were moving out the state.

We moved to Douglasville, Georgia, because I and the father of my other children decided to work things out. He transferred his job to Georgia, so I had to follow him. At the time, I couldn't transfer my job because the location in Georgia was too far from where we lived. I put them in school and found another job closer to home.

It was Stacey's senior year of high school. We had to prepare for the senior prom and graduation. She was very smart in school and very intelligent. She was driving her own car since the age of fourteen, a Honda Accord that she was so happy with. In high school, she wanted another car, so we got her a Malibu. She didn't like it at first, but she couldn't find the car she really wanted and the ones she found were out of our price range. She and her friends would drive to school, while the other kids rode the bus, or I drove them myself. She didn't even let her brother Rico ride with her, and he was only a year younger than she. Of course, you know how that goes. I would have to drive him to school.

Well, I had some major situations going on in my life and they lead me back to Mississippi. It left Stacey and me in a bad situation, because she would graduate a few weeks later and I couldn't pull her out of school. So, a friend of mine said that Stacey could live with her and finish her senior year in Georgia. This friend of mine had a son, and he and Stacey started dating.

It was graduation day and we were all in Mississippi trying to make it to

Douglasville on time. We were driving seventy five to eighty miles an hour, three car loads of us. We finally made it there. Although we were late, we were just in time to see her walk and receive Stacey diploma. Yes! I cried, because it was along hard journey to make sure she succeeded in life. I said once again, "Thank you God... Thank you for seeing me through. Nobody said that this would be easy, but we made it through."

High school graduation was over and I thought Stacey was going directly into college and join the arm, but she proceeded to tell me that she was going put everything off until the next semester. I was really angry with Stacey. I was very upset with her decision. She wanted to move in with her boyfriend and get a job. I didn't like it at all, but she was grown and could make her own decisions, right or wrong.

Some months later Stacey became pregnant and tried to work at the same time. Of course, he worked as well. I didn't like it, but they seemed to be getting along okay; so I left it alone. It wasn't until later that I found out he was putting his hands on her and fighting her. My family and I loaded up in a few cars headed to Georgia to straighten him out. We ended up getting into it with his entire family. It was a big altercation that escalated quickly. She decided to put him out of the apartment, but it wasn't long before her love for him conquered the entire situation and she took him back. I stepped down again and began to let them deal with their problems on their own. It wasn't long after the big dispute that she gave birth to her first child. We all had to load up again and head to Georgia to be there when the baby came. We missed the birth of the baby, because we were all at the apartment asleep, and she dilated faster than the doctors could imagine.

When we arrived, Stacey had already given birth to my first grandchild, "Justice Dekalen-Justice Waller." She was very beautiful, with a head full of hair. I knew she too would be very spoiled; she was and still is! So now my daughter is a mother and I was proud of her. I know that Stacey can achieve anything she puts her mind to; she has what it takes to succeed in this world.

Stacey has conquered and overcome a lot of struggles in life, where many young women failed. She picked herself up and fought back, leaving those who tried to destroy her innocence, feeling shameless and looking stupid. All of the fake people that were her friends and turned into foes disgusted me at times. If she can move on and forgive them, then I'll fall in line and back her up. Just like me, she will never forget what they've done to her, but God knows best. We just have to continue to know our place in life and he will take care of the rest. Never take matters into your own hand, is what I always try to apply. The battle is not yours, but it's the Lord. Seek and you will find, and that's what Stacey has done. She has found the Lord and found her way through life, out of all the stumbling blocks that were laid out for her to fall over. She has fallen at time, but God has always helped her get back up, shake it off, and move on. With this being said, I say to you my child, "Well done. Currently, you are raising three children on your own, a single mom with dreams still bigger than life. I pray this book brings you plenty of success and financial stability. May God keep you lifted before him, and let your blessings continue to flow."

Sincerely,

A mother's love

14 From a Sister's Eyes

My view...

As the middle child of seven kids, attention was fairly hard to get. I often kept to myself, which is the best way to be, at least that's what I thought. Of all my mother's children, only three stood in the center of attention: Stacey, Rico, and Lola. As you must know, Stacey is the eldest of us all. Everything revolved around her and her needs. Next was Rico, who is the second oldest and worse child in the family. He stayed in trouble and anytime he was in trouble my mama would break her neck to get him out of it, which is why I feel like he is in his situation now. The youngest child is Lola, the favorite to everyone. She was supposed to be the beauty queen of the family.

My family supported everything Stacey and Lola did. Stacey wanted to be a cheerleader and she had all the support she needed. If she wanted a new car she would get it. I looked at my family often like "What the hell is this?" I wasn't a cheerleader or a beauty queen. I just loved to do hair, that was my only passion, but trouble was what I knew best. I couldn't complete anything in school because I was at home a majority of the time.

I was the complete opposite of my siblings. Stacey was the type that would make fun of others. She was also bossy. As a child, I thought Stacey was smart and pretty. As years passed, I began to hate her. She would always talk bad about us and towards us when her friends came around; by us, I mean all her siblings. As long as she had a car, I can never remember riding in it unless I was stealing it. She would make a fool of her friends more often than anyone could imagine. In order for them to ride in her front seat, somebody had to give her something that benefited her; life appeared to be perfect for her.

We moved to Georgia and she started hanging with a few ghetto, hood rats. Not long after that, she started stealing and doing other things. She ended up costing my momma a lot of money and more heartache. She started hanging out later and later, her grades began to slip, and she seemed to be giving up on the important things in her life. "Where did this drastic change come from," is the question everyone was asking. As expected, it was the fact she that she was dating this guy Juan who moved to Georgia from Detroit shortly after we did. Her head was so far in the clouds, if it rained, she would have drowned. They were always with each other.

Stacey became pregnant with her first child not long after. Would you be surprised to find out that's when his true colors began to show? This girl was so popular and sadiddy, but this abusive man began to make her feel the complete opposite. You can tell that he was taking her through hell, because it began to show in her face. It was easy to see the hurt and embarrassment she felt as if she was wearing it as clothing. As much as she did for him and his family, who would have ever thought he would have been the one to change her whole perspective of men. Since then, every man that wants to or has pursued her has gotten no respect. I believe God allowed her to go through that awful relationship, so she would be able to appreciate her past lessons. Sometimes you have to go through the bad to appreciate what's good. His abuse was her motivation to help other girls who might be in a similar situation.

15 In My Baby Sister's Words

I am one of the youngest of my mother's seven kids. My brother Money and I are twins, also the last to join the family. Growing up as the youngest was not easy, especially with a big sister like mines. Stacey really made my life a living hell, yet I always wanted to be around her. Coming from our background we're very familiar with the term "tough love." I was usually sick a lot as a child, and with it being so many of us, my sister had to step up at a young age to help my mother take care of us.

Stacey always told my mom, "I don't want to stay here and watch these ugly kids, huh!" So, when she had to be forced to watch us, she would sneak and pinch me and say, "You'd better not tell or I'm not going to give you any of my snacks." I would cry and later she would give me some of her snacks, and I would be happy again. We're not your typical family but we are all very close. We've cried together, fought together, and struggled together. We have endured pain lots of children don't experience until their adulthood and for those reasons, we are stronger today.

I take my hat off to my sister, because she has been through so much and still finds room in her heart to keep pushing and accomplish things so we as a family can have a better life. She is a go-getter, meaning she's going to keep striving until she makes it to the top. There is no sitting on her ass; she's all about her business. With a past like hers, I can't do anything but respect her. You see she now walks in my mother's footsteps, the single mother of three kids with no help from their fathers. Like I said, we are a family so I help out as much as possible.

I love my niece and nephews beyond my control. After losing my only child, I began to see a part of her in each one of them. Now I love them even harder. I might be the youngest, but I protect my family with every part of me. I watched one of the fathers of my sister's children hit her while she was pregnant. "Ha, ha," I hope he really didn't think I was just going to sit there; I beat his ass and I will do it again. I don't play about my sister, even though she gets on my nerves most of the time. My sister and I grew a lot closer after that and became closer when we had our little girls on the same day, March 2, 2010. I count it as a blessing to be able to finally share something with my older sister besides her snacks. We as a family will continue to grow stronger every day. With me, she will always have a shoulder to lean on. I wish for her the best that life itself has to offer. I know she will keep going further.

16 Help For Transformations

A lot of people are stunned by the fact of me making a complete 180 with my life. But they don't know that this change in my life has nothing to do with me. Even I was stunned by the way my life began to transform from the unhappy, bitter, grudge holding Stacey with the bad attitude, to this newly refined, bright eyed light, who has allowed the power of God to come in and completely redefine me. I have always been a prayer warrior, even when I had little faith in God. The amazing thing about this drastic change in me was similar to the scripture in the bible when it stated that "God would be coming back like a thief in the night." That's exactly what he did when he intervened in my life and took control. That moment in August 2012 when I was walking to the alter for the hundredth time, for some reason I knew that this would be my last time repenting, because I was disgusted with the woman I'd become and the life I lived. I cried out to God begging for forgiveness and another chance to do his will, his way! That very moment, with tears flowing down my face like rainfall, he intervened and touched me. The Holy Ghost was all over me. I couldn't do anything, but cry, cry, and cry. It was an amazing feeling! After coming back to myself, nothing in me felt the same. It was like my mind and heart were wiped clean, as if they were completely brand new! I was so happy. My spirit was happy. I know that the peace and love I have now is not because of me and my capabilities, but God and his love for me. I have been called to do the will of God, and that's all I want to do.

_____
_____
_____
_____
_____
_____
_____
_____
_____
_____
_____
_____
_____
_____
_____
_____
_____
_____
_____
_____
_____
_____
_____
_____
_____
_____
_____
_____
_____
_____
_____
_____

Ezekiel 18:30 "Therefore I will judge you, O house of Israel, every one according to his ways, saith the Lord GOD. Repent, and turn yourselves from all your transgressions; so iniquity shall not be your ruin."

"I began to reformat my mind and the things I entertained."

_____
_____
_____
_____
_____
_____
_____
_____
_____
_____
_____
_____
_____
_____
_____
_____
_____
_____
_____
_____
_____
_____
_____
_____
_____
_____
_____
_____
_____
_____

Philippians 4:8 "Finally, brethren, whatsoever things are true, whatsoever things are honest, whatsoever things are just, whatsoever things are pure, whatsoever things are lovely, whatsoever things are of good report; if there be any virtue, and if there be any praise, think on these things."

"I began to remove negative people and things out of my life."

Proverbs 12:26 "The righteous is more excellent than his neighbour: but the way of the wicked seduceth them."

"I stop doing things that I knew was wrong."

Psalms 34:14 "Depart from evil, and do good: seek peace and pursue it."

"I started declaring respect about myself and for myself."

_____
_____
_____
_____
_____
_____
_____
_____
_____
_____
_____
_____
_____
_____
_____
_____
_____
_____
_____
_____
_____
_____
_____
_____
_____
_____
_____
_____
_____
_____
_____
_____
_____
_____
_____

1 Corinthians 6:20 "For ye are bought with a price: therefore glorify God in your body, and in your spirit, which are God's."

"I began to view life with a new pair of eyes."

_____

_____
_____
_____
_____
_____
_____
_____
_____
_____
_____
_____
_____
_____
_____
_____
_____
_____
_____
_____
_____
_____
_____
_____
_____
_____
_____
_____
_____
_____
_____
_____

Psalm 119:18 "Open thou mine eyes, that I may behold wondrous things out of thy law."

"It wasn't easy changing.
I knew that in order for God to make the necessary steps in my life, I would have to take certain steps."

_____
_____
_____
_____
_____
_____
_____
_____
_____
_____
_____
_____
_____
_____
_____
_____
_____
_____
_____
_____
_____
_____
_____
_____
_____
_____
_____
_____
_____
_____
_____
_____
_____
_____
_____

Psalms 37:23 "The steps of a good man are ordered by the LORD: and he delighteth in his way."

"I was afraid of falling again, afraid that things will not get better but worse if I tried. For so long I have allowed the spirit of fear to roam around in my life and hold me hostage! That even if I someone told me, 'You can do it,' I didn't believe them. I didn't even believe in myself."

Hebrews 13:6 "So that we may boldly say, The Lord is my helper, and I will not fear what man shall do unto me."

"My whole life has been filled with challenges and struggles, and for years I allowed my past to dictate my future; not any longer."

_____
_____
_____
_____
_____
_____
_____
_____
_____
_____
_____
_____
_____
_____
_____
_____
_____
_____
_____
_____
_____
_____
_____
_____
_____
_____
_____
_____
_____
_____
_____

Philippians 3:13-14 "Brothers, I do not consider that I have made it my own. But one thing I do: forgetting what lies behind and straining forward to what lies ahead, I press on toward the goal for the prize of the upward call of God in Christ Jesus."

"It was hard work transforming myself into this positive, high spirited, dream seeking woman. God is the key."

2 Corinthians 5:17 "Therefore if any man be in Christ, he is a new creature: old things are passed away; behold, all things are become new."

ABOUT THE AUTHOR

Laqulia Shinn graduated high school at Douglas County High School, in Douglasville, Georgia in May of 2004. She is currently attending Meridian Community College pursuing her Associates Degree in Psychology and hopes to graduate spring of 2014. Stacey is also the Founder of the newly implemented "Rising Star's All-Girl Youth Ministry" in her hometown of Columbus, Mississippi. Although she faced bad things in her life, she still finds it in her to keep walking through the storms. As she likes to say, "In order to tell a story, you have to be a story, AND I AM A LIVING TESTIMONY" of what God can do when you really surrender all to him.

www.ingramcontent.com/pod-product-compliance
Lightning Source LLC
Chambersburg PA
CBHW060635280326
41933CB00012B/2049